EARTH'S CONTINENTS

Australia

by Mary Lindeen

Australia is the smallest **continent** in the world. It is also the only continent that is its own **country**.

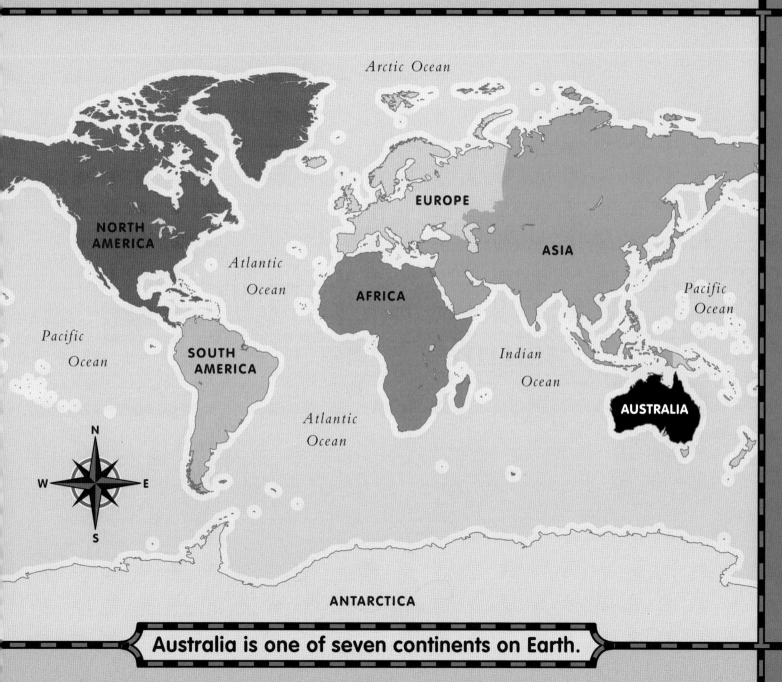

Arctic Ocean

NORTH
AMERICA

EUROPE

ASIA

Atlantic
Ocean

AFRICA

Pacific
Ocean

Pacific
Ocean

SOUTH
AMERICA

Indian
Ocean

AUSTRALIA

Atlantic
Ocean

N

W   E

S

ANTARCTICA

Australia is one of seven continents on Earth.

Australia is between the Indian Ocean and the Pacific Ocean. It is near many small Pacific **islands**. It is also near the continent of Antarctica.

The Byron Bay in Australia leads to the Pacific Ocean.

Australia is very flat and dry.
Most of Australia is desert
and dry **grassland**.

Grasslands are common in Australia.

The desert area in the center of Australia is called the outback. Not many people live there.

The outback gets very little rain.

The outback used to be home to **Aborigines**.* These people were experts at living in the desert. Today, ranchers raise cattle and sheep in the outback.

*Say it! *ab-uh-RIJ-uh-neez*

Aborigines painted these figures on rocks thousands of years ago.

Most people in Australia live in big cities near the **coastline**. Sydney is one well-known city.

About four million people live in Sydney, Australia.

Australia is known for its beautiful beaches. Many people come to see the Great Barrier Reef. It is the largest **coral reef** in the world.

The Great Barrier Reef is located along the northeast coast of Australia.

Australia is also home to interesting animals such as koalas and kangaroos. Koalas are only found in Australia.

Koalas spend most of their lives in trees.

Australia has many amazing things to see in nature. Ayers Rock has small caves covered with Aborigines' wall paintings.

Ayers Rock is a popular site in Australia.

Australia also has many human-made things to see. Which part of Australia is the most interesting to you?

Flinders Street Station is a well-known railway station in Australia.

Glossary

Aborigines (ab-uh-RIJ-uh-neez): Aborigines are the first people to ever live in Australia. The Aborigines lived in the outback.

coastline (KOHST-line): A coastline is the spot where the ocean meets land. Sydney is a big Australian city near the coastline.

continent (KON-tuh-nent): A continent is one of seven large land areas on Earth. Australia is a continent.

coral reef (KOR-ull REEF): A reef is a ridge that sticks up from the ocean floor. Coral looks like colorful rocks but it is made of the skeletons of small sea creatures and other materials. The largest coral reef in the world is located off the coast of Australia.

country (KUN-tree): A country is an area of land with its own government. Australia is both a continent and a country.

grassland (GRASS-land): A grassland is a large open area of grass where animals can graze. In Australia, cattle graze on grassland.

islands (EYE-lands): Islands are areas of land surrounded by water. Australia is near many Pacific islands.

To Find Out More

Books

Bancroft, Bronwyn. *Patterns of Australia*. Sydney, Australia: Little Hare Books, 2006.

Kalman, Bobbie, and Robin Johnson. *Koalas and Other Marsupials*. New York: Crabtree Publishing, 2005.

McLeod, Kate. *Outback Adventure: Australian Vacation*. New York: DK Children, 2004.

Web Sites

Visit our Web site for links about Australia:
childsworld.com/links

Note to Parents, Teachers, and Librarians: We routinely verify our Web links to make sure they are safe and active sites. So encourage your readers to check them out!

Index

About the Author

Mary Lindeen is an elementary school teacher who turned her love of children and books into a career in publishing. She has written and edited many library books and literacy programs. She also enjoys traveling with her son, Benjamin, whenever and wherever she can.

On the cover: Kangaroos live in Australia.

Published by The Child's World®
1980 Lookout Drive • Mankato, MN 56003-1705
800-599-READ • www.childsworld.com

ACKNOWLEDGMENTS
The Child's World®: Mary Berendes, Publishing Director
The Design Lab: Design, page, and map production
Red Line Editorial: Editorial direction

PHOTO CREDITS: James Thew/iStockphoto, cover; Ximagination/
Shutterstock, 5; YoavPeled/Shutterstock, 7; Sander van Sinttruye/
Shutterstock, 9; Sam DCruz/Shutterstock, 11; Debra James/
Shutterstock, 13, 15; Renate Micallef/Shutterstock, 17; thisorder/
Shutterstock, 19; flavia bottazzini/iStockphoto, 21.

Printed in the United States of America in Mankato, Minnesota.
November 2009
F11460

LIBRARY OF CONGRESS CATALOGING-IN-PUBLICATION DATA
Lindeen, Mary.
 Australia : by Mary Lindeen.
  p. cm. — (Earth's continents)
 Includes index.
 ISBN 978-1-60253-349-3 (library bound : alk. paper)
 1. Australia—Juvenile literature. I. Title. II. Series.
 DU96.L56 2010
 994—dc22   2009030010